Will Smith

The Funny, Funky, and Confident Fresh Prince

by Eric Embacher

Reading Consultant:
Timothy Rasinski, Ph.D.
Professor of Reading Education
Kent State University

Content Consultant:
George Thomas
Entertainment Writer
The Akron Beacon Journal

Red Brick™ Learning

Published by Red Brick™ Learning
7825 Telegraph Road, Bloomington, Minnesota 55438
http://www.redbricklearning.com

Library of Congress Cataloging-in-Publication Data
Embacher, Eric, 1975–
> Will Smith : the funny, funky, and confident fresh prince / by Eric
> Embacher.
> p. cm.
> Summary: Follows the career of Will Smith, from young rapper to
television star to movie superstar, emphasizing his sense of humor, drive, talent,
confidence, family relationships, and personal growth.
> Includes bibliographical references and index.
> ISBN 0-7368-2786-2 (Hardcover); ISBN 0-7368-2829-X (Paperback)
> 1. Smith, Will, 1968—Juvenile literature. 2. Actors—United States—
Biography—Juvenile literature. 3. Rap musicians—United States—Biography—
Juvenile literature. [1. Smith, Will, 1968- 2. Actors and actresses. 3. Musicians.
4. Rap (Music) 5. African Americans--Biography.]
I. Title.
PN2287.S612E43 2003
791.43'028'092—dc21

2003006338

Created by Kent Publishing Services, Inc.
Designed by Signature Design Group, Inc.
This publisher has made every effort to trace ownership of all copyrighted
material and to secure necessary permissions. In the event of any questions
arising as to the use of any material, the publisher, while expressing regret for
any inadvertent error, will be happy to make necessary corrections.

Photo Credits:
Cover, Debbie VanStory, iPhoto/NewsCom; page 4, Bettmann/Corbis;
page 7, Fred Prouser/Reuters New Media, Inc./Corbis; page 9, Columbia
Pictures/Zuma Press; page 10, Mychal Watts/Wireimage; page 13, Nick
Elgar/Sygma/Corbis; pages 17, 21, 23, Neal Preston/Corbis; pages 18, 27, 29,
31, Sygma/Corbis; page 20, Mitchell Gerber/Corbis; page 24, Howard
Jacqueline/Corbis; page 32, Annamaria Disanto/Wireimage; page 33,
Robert Millard, Zuma Press; page 35, Bob King/Wireimage; page 36, Lucy
Nicholson/AFP/Corbis; page 39, Gregory Pace/Corbis; page 41, Photographers
Showcase/NewsCom; page 43, Columbia Pictures/Zuma Press

Printed in the United States of America.

2 3 4 5 6 08 07 06 05

Table of Contents

Chapter 1: Lights, Camera, Action! . 4

Chapter 2: A New Music 10

Chapter 3: Will Needs a New Job . 18

Chapter 4: Hitting the Big Screen . . 24

Chapter 5: The Future 36

Epilogue 40

Time Line 42

Glossary 44

Bibliography 46

Useful Addresses 47

Internet Sites 47

Index 48

Lights, Camera, Action!

Blood and sweat lie in little pools all over the ring. Two boxers stare at each other. They begin to circle, throwing short punches. Each is looking for an opening. Each wants to throw the "big punch" that will end the match. Each wants to leave the ring as champ.

Two boxers look for the big punch.

The Match

Muhammad Ali (moh-HA-muhd ah-LEE) is hurting. His face is swollen. He can hardly see. But he is still standing. So is the champ.

Ali gathers his strength. He rushes the champ. Ali **lands** punches to his head and body. The champ is **dazed**. The bell rings. Ali walks back to his corner.

The next round begins. Ali is ready for more. But the champ doesn't stand up. He has given up! Ali has won! He is the new heavyweight champion of the world! Ali raises his gloves in victory. He dances around the ring, yelling, "I am the greatest!"

"Cut!" yells the **director**. "That was great, Will! Let's do it one more time."

---

land: to strike a blow
daze: to stun or confuse
director: the person in charge of making a play, a movie, or a radio or television program

A Visit from the Real Ali

Will Smith looked beaten and bruised. He had just filmed a fight scene for his new movie, *Ali*. It took five days to film just 32 seconds of one fight scene.

Will was acting as the famous boxer, Muhammad Ali, in the movie. Will had to learn how to box to play this role. One day, the real Ali came to help. Will was thrilled. He tried to do his best Ali **impersonation** for the past champ. He jumped around the ring. He waved his arms. He screamed, "You ain't pretty enough to be in here with me. You takin' away from my pretty!"

Ali was **impressed**. He said to a friend, "Man, how come you [didn't] tell me how crazy I was when I was young?" For Will, Ali's words were the highest **compliment**.

---

impersonation: a copy or imitation of someone's actions
impress: to have a strong effect on someone's mind
compliment: something said to praise another

Looking for a Challenge

Will didn't have to act in a movie that was so hard as *Ali*. He was already a superstar. He could have picked a movie that needed less training, less work.

But Will likes **challenges**. He wants to become a better actor. This **drive** has led him through an exciting and successful career. But it has also been tough at times.

Will learned many values growing up that have helped him. Two of those values are to work hard and to keep a sense of humor.

---

challenge: something difficult that takes extra effort to do
drive: the power or energy to get things done

Life Growing Up

Will grew up in a fairly average family. Both of Will's parents worked. Will's father was strict and taught Will to be a hard worker. His mother was gentle and **supportive**.

One thing the Smiths did was to laugh a lot. Will says, "Dinnertime was like a nightly laugh riot."

This family humor helped prepare Will to become an **entertainer**. He knew how to make people laugh.

First Music Lessons

Will took his first music lessons from his parents. He began with the piano. Next, he chose the drums. He loved making **rhythms** and beats. This early learning helped get him started in music.

---

supportive: encouraging; helpful
entertainer: a person who performs for people
rhythm: the movement or flow of sounds in a pattern

School Days

Will also did well in school. He especially enjoyed English and poetry.

Will was a happy child. He had a funny, loving family. He liked to read and make music. But he had no idea where all this might lead him.

Will acts in the movie, Ali.

CHAPTER 2

A New Music

Will Smith was 12 years old when he first heard a rap song. It was "Rapper's Delight," by the Sugar Hill Gang. Will was amazed. The words were like poetry. The performers spoke them over a strong beat and rhythm. Will couldn't wait to hear more!

The Sugar Hill Gang

Rap and Hip-Hop

What Will heard that day was one of the very first rap hits. Like many teens in the early '80s, Will came to love rap. In a few years, he began to act as **DJ** at his friends' parties. He played rap and hip-hop music.

Will Begins to Rap

Will liked rap music so much, he started to perform it. He liked to get into rap "street battles." That's where two rappers try to "out-rap" each other. Will could always come up with clever **lyrics**. He never lost. Soon, people began to ask Will to rap at parties.

"Now what you hear is not a test, I'm rappin' to the beat.
And me, the groove, and my friends are gonna try to move your feet.
See I am wonder Mike, and I'd like to say hello
To the black, to the white, the red, and the brown, the purple, and yellow."

— from "Rapper's Delight"

DJ: disc jockey; a person who plays recorded music
lyric: the words of a song

Will Meets DJ Jazzy Jeff

In 1981, Jeff Townes was a DJ in Philadelphia. One night, he was playing at a party on Will's block. Will asked Jeff if he could rap while Jeff played music.

That night Jeff blasted music through the speakers and Will rapped. The crowd loved it.

Will and Jeff worked well with each other. Each one seemed to know what the other was going to do next—Will with words, and Jeff with music.

DJ Jazzy Jeff and The Fresh Prince

Will and Jeff began to write and record music together. Jeff was a DJ, and he loved jazz. So he became "DJ Jazzy Jeff." Will could talk his way out of anything at school. His teachers called him "Prince **Charming**." Will dropped the "Charming" and added "Fresh." So he became "The Fresh Prince."

---

charming: very pleasing to others; attractive

DJ Jazzy Jeff and The Fresh Prince

The First Single

Will's parents **insisted** he do well in school. Then he could rap all he wanted. Will agreed. During Will's senior year of high school, Will and Jeff signed a **recording contract**. Their first **single** was called "Girls Ain't Nuthin' But Trouble."

A Huge Success

Most rap music at this time was about drugs and gangs. Will and Jeff's song was different. It was about teen love. The song was a huge hit. The single sold more than 100,000 copies. DJ Jazzy Jeff and The Fresh Prince were stars!

In 1988, Jeff and Will made a new album. It was called, *He's the DJ, I'm the Rapper*. The album was a big success. It sold more than 3 million copies.

---

insist: to demand something very firmly
recording contract: an agreement to record music for a fee
single: a recording having one short tune on each side

Jeff and Will Win a Grammy

The album, *He's the DJ, I'm the Rapper*, had a song titled, "Parents Just Don't Understand." The song is about a teen who is dealing with his un-cool parents. The teen's mother wants to buy him clothes from the 1970s. It's a funny song and fans loved it. The song won the first-ever **Grammy** award for rap.

"You know parents are the same,
No matter time or place.
They don't understand that us kids,
Are gonna make some mistakes.
So to you, all the kids, all across the land.
There's no need to argue,
Parents just don't understand."

—from "Parents Just Don't Understand"

Grammy: a prize awarded in the recording industry

Rich, Then Broke

Will was suddenly rich. He bought a **mansion** and six cars. He wore a diamond and gold necklace that spelled "Fresh Prince." He bought lots of clothes. He spent more than $800,000 in one year. He saved nothing.

Then one day, Will received a letter from the U.S. government. The letter said he owed more than $1 million in taxes. Will sold most of what he owned. But he still did not have enough money to pay the taxes. He went from being rich to being broke. Will said, "There's nothing [like] having six cars and a mansion one day and you can't even buy gas for the cars the next."

What was Will going to do? Could he and Jeff make another hit album? Could Will find some other way to make a living? What would you do?

---

mansion: a very large house

16

*Will sits on the roof
of one of his six cars.*

CHAPTER 3

Will Needs a New Job

Will was broke. His third album, In This Corner, *was not selling well. Fans were losing interest in Will and Jeff's rap style. Will thought about making a new album. But that might not sell well, either.*

Will Smith and the cast of
The Fresh Prince of Bel-Air

A Lucky Meeting

In 1989, Will met a TV **producer** named Benny Medina in Los Angeles. Medina told Will about an idea for a new TV show.

The new show was about a young African American man from the inner city who moves in with a rich family near Hollywood. Medina thought Will might be right for the part. They agreed to talk more.

A few months later, Will tried out for the part. Will had never acted before. But he impressed Medina and the other producers. He was charming and funny. Medina wanted to take a chance. He gave Will the lead role in *The Fresh Prince of Bel-Air*.

---

producer: a person who oversees or pays to create a TV show or film

A Rough Start

At first, Will was a poor
actor. A younger actress on
the show, Tatyana Ali, said,
"I couldn't believe what a
bad actor he was."

Tatyana Ali

It was a hard time for
Will. He was worried the
show would not do well.
To help, Will went all over the country
to **promote** *The Fresh Prince of Bel-Air*.
Will said, "My **motivation** is that I hate not
being on top." He wanted to do whatever it
took for the show to be successful.

A Big Hit

In the end, all the hard work paid off.
After a few months, *The Fresh Prince of Bel-
Air* was the top show in its **time slot**. Later,
The Fresh Prince of Bel-Air ranked as high as
14th among the top 80 shows on TV.

---

promote: to tell others about something in order to sell it
motivation: the will to do something
time slot: the period of time when a TV show is broadcast

Will Smith on the set of The Fresh Prince of Bel-Air

Big Improvement

Will's charm made up for his acting mistakes. But his acting also improved. In the show's second year, Will was even **nominated** for a Best Actor award. He did not win the award, called a Golden Globe. But the TV **network** was thrilled.

Will was thrilled as well. After his struggles, Will was again a success. But this time, he was a success as an actor, not a rapper. Over the next six years, *The Fresh Prince of Bel-Air* made 149 shows. It also made Will Smith a rich TV star.

---

nominate: to name someone for an award or a position
network: a radio or television company that produces programs for broadcast

Will Smith was nominated for a Best Actor award for his role in The Fresh Prince of Bel-Air.

Chapter 4

Hitting the Big Screen

Will was a successful rapper. He had a hit TV show. But he wasn't through. Will wanted to act in movies. Soon, he got his chance.

In 1992, Will Smith had a small role in the film Made in America.

Small Roles First

After the first season of *The Fresh Prince of Bel-Air*, Will wanted to act in movies. He said he hoped to begin with small roles. Then he could learn more about making movies before he took a larger role.

For his first movie part, Will played a homeless teen in a wheelchair. The movie was called *Where the Day Takes You*. It had a big effect on Will. He said, "Just seeing how people ignore the homeless was an amazing lesson."

Will got good **reviews** for his small role. Over the next few years, he took other small roles in films. He did this during his breaks from *The Fresh Prince of Bel-Air*.

---

review: a piece of writing or a TV or radio report that gives an opinion about a new book, movie, play, etc.

First Big Movie Role

In the summer of 1995, the movie *Bad Boys* opened. It starred Will Smith and Martin Lawrence. Will had fun making the movie. The two actors often made up their own lines as they acted. Will said, "It was two and a half months of two of the silliest guys in **comedy** doing exactly what they wanted to."

The movie was a big hit, thanks in part to Will's acting. It also made Will a well-known movie actor. But his next movie would make him even more famous.

---

comedy: a play, movie, or TV show that is funny and usually has a happy ending

Martin Lawrence and Will Smith in Bad Boys

Independence Day

The next summer, Will starred in *Independence Day*, a movie about **aliens** attacking Earth. Will played a funny fighter pilot. "I want to play characters that **represent** really strong, positive black images," Will said about the role.

Much of the movie was filmed in the desert. Some days were as hot as 126 degrees Fahrenheit (52 degrees Celsius). Will worked hard. He also kept everyone's spirits up by making them laugh.

Independence Day set a record when it opened. The film made more than $50 million its first weekend. After two months, the movie had already made close to $300 million. Will said, "The day before *Independence Day* opened, people on the street were like, 'Will, what's up?' The day after, it was, 'Hey, Mr. Smith, how are you?' There's a whole diffcrent level of **respect**."

---

alien: a being from outer space
represent: to show
respect: a feeling of honor or regard

Men In Black

The next offer that Will liked came from the famous movie director and producer, Steven Spielberg. Spielberg asked Will to co-star in the movie *Men In Black*. Will agreed. As Will said, "You don't say no to Steven Spielberg."

Will Smith holds an alien in the movie Men In Black.

A Messy Situation

Men In Black was also a movie about aliens. Will played a secret police officer. His job was to watch for aliens that are breaking the law.

In the movie's final scene, Will and his partner destroy an evil alien. But first the alien covers them in slime. To make this scene, the director used buckets of goo and wet noodles. Will said, "It got in your ears and nose and hair, 12 hours a day, for three days."

In the end, all the slime and goo was worth it. *Men In Black* set a new record by earning $51 million the weekend it opened.

Will Smith and
Tommy Lee Jones
starred in the hit
movie, Men In Black.

Time to Rap Again

Will wanted to get back to making music. He started by recording a **theme song** for *Men In Black*. That song became a big hit.

Later, Will finished a new album, *Big Willie Style*. It was Will's first album in six years. It was also his most successful! The album had a string of hits. Besides "Men In Black" it included "Gettin' Jiggy Wit It," "Just the Two of Us," and "Miami." Will Smith, the rap artist, was back!

Will returns to rap.

---

theme song: the main song in a movie, play, or TV show

Back to Movies

Will followed *Men In Black* with more **dramatic** movies. This gave Will the chance to become a more **versatile** and respected actor. Producers now offered Will roles that were both funny and dramatic. Either way, the producers knew people would come to see a movie starring Will Smith.

Will signs autographs.

---

dramatic: full of action or drama
versatile: changing easily

Ali—Will's Toughest Role

Many people think Muhammad Ali was the best heavyweight boxer ever. He had great power, speed, and skill. He also was **outspoken**, loud, and **confident**. Still today, Ali is famous all over the world. Who could play the part of Ali in a movie? Will wanted to give it a try. But he also had doubts.

First, Will was skinny. He did not have the **muscular** body of a boxer. Second, he was almost too well known himself to **portray** Ali. People knew Will for his comedy role as the "Fresh Prince." Would people believe him as the **fearsome** heavyweight champ? No one was sure. But the film's director wanted Will to play Ali. Will took the part.

Now, Will wanted to prove he could do it. As Will once said, "I hate—refuse—to lose."

---

outspoken: speaking in a bold way
confident: sure or certain
muscular: made up of large muscles
portray: to play the role of; to act as
fearsome: scary

Success, Again

Will lifted weights and learned to box. He fought in real boxing matches. He studied films of Ali's fights. He wanted to move just like Ali in the ring. He studied how Ali talked. He wanted to sound just like him, too.

Once again, Will's hard work paid off. He received an **Oscar** nomination for his role as Ali. Will did not win the award. But to be nominated is a great **honor.** Will Smith had succeeded again.

Will poses before the opening of the movie Ali.

Oscar: an award given to actors, directors, designers, etc.
honor: an award or credit

— CHAPTER 5 —

The Future

Today, Will Smith has a family he loves. He has a career in TV, movies, and music. What more can Will do? Even he is not sure. But Will says it is going to be something big.

Will Smith and his family dressed up for the opening of his movie, Wild Wild West.

Family Man

Will married Hollywood actress Jada Pinkett in 1997. Since then, he has been a **devoted** family man. He enjoys spending time with his wife, his sons, Trey and Jaden, and his daughter, Willow.

On his album, *Big Willie Style*, Will wrote a song about his son Trey. "Just the Two of Us" is about Will's feelings for his newborn son. The song was even made into a children's book, also called *Just the Two of Us.*

Early in 2002, Will again showed that family comes first. Will and his wife were enjoying themselves at the Oscar award show. But he and Jada left early. They went home because their daughter was sick.

---

devoted: very loving or loyal

Bright Future

Will's future looks bright. In 2002, he released another album, *Born to Reign*. He also starred in the **sequel** to *Men In Black*, called *Men In Black II*.

Will is not sure what he will do next. He said he believes he is "heading for something bigger." He just doesn't know yet what that might be.

Will is confident that he can **accomplish** anything he wants to. "I absolutely believe I could be the president of the United States," Will once said. "I believe that if that's what I wanted to do with my life, I could win."

---

sequel: the next movie or book in a series
accomplish: to achieve or do

Will has many reasons to smile.

39

Epilogue

Set Apart from the Crowd

Rap music often uses words that shock and even **offend** many people. Will won't do that.

Will decided as a young man to use clean language. He said that at first he "used **expletives** and four-letter words, because that's what rap was. My grandmother got ahold of my rap book, read it, and wrote in the back: 'Dear Willard, truly **intelligent** people do not have to use these types of words to express themselves.' We never talked about it, but from that day on, I didn't use those words." Will is now teaching his own children this lesson.

---

offend: to make someone feel hurt or angry
expletive: a swear word
intelligent: smart

Nothing Less Than the Best

Throughout his career, Will has shown a great deal of drive. He has worked hard to earn the respect and awards he has received.

Will said, "If it's a record, I want it to be number one. If it's a film, I want it to **translate** to every single person on the planet. I've always measured success by how many people I reach."

---

translate: to put into words other people can understand

1968—September 25 – Willard C. Smith, Jr. is born.

1986—Will and Jeff release their first album, *Rock the House*.

1987—Will and DJ Jazzy Jeff release their first single, "Girls Ain't Nuthin' But Trouble."

1988—Will and Jeff release their second album, the double album, *He's the DJ, I'm the Rapper*.

1989—Will and Jeff receive the first ever Grammy award for a rap song.

1989—Will receives a letter from the U.S. government saying he owes $1 million in taxes.

1990—Will joins the cast of a new TV show, *The Fresh Prince of Bel-Air*.

1992—Will has his first movie role, in *Where the Day Takes You*.

1992—Will is nominated for a Golden Globe award for Best Actor in a Comedy for *The Fresh Prince of Bel-Air*.

1995—Will has his first movie lead, in *Bad Boys*.

1996—Will has his first blockbuster, *Independence Day*.

1997—Will leads *Men In Black* to record earnings.

1997—Will releases his first rap album in six years, *Big Willie Style*.

1997—Will wins an MTV Video Music Award—Best
Video from a Film—for *Men In Black*.

1997—Will marries Jada Pinkett.

1998—Will wins a Grammy award for Best Rap Solo
Performance for "Men In Black."

1999—Will wins an MTV Video Music Award—Best
Male Video—for "Miami."

2001—Will stars in *Ali*.

2002—Will is nominated for an Oscar for Best Actor for
his role as Muhammad Ali in *Ali*.

Glossary

accomplish: to achieve or do

alien: a being from outer space

challenge: something difficult that takes extra effort to do

charming: very pleasing to others; attractive

comedy: a play, movie, or TV show that is funny and usually has a happy ending

compliment: something said to praise another

confident: sure or certain

daze: to stun or confuse

devoted: very loving or loyal

director: the person in charge of making a play, a movie, or a radio or television program

DJ: disc jockey; a person who plays recorded music

dramatic: full of action or drama

drive: the power or energy to get things done

entertainer: a person who performs for people

expletive: a swear word

fearsome: scary

Grammy: a prize awarded in the recording industry

honor: an award or credit

impersonation: a copy or imitation of someone's actions

impress: to have a strong effect on someone's mind

insist: to demand something very firmly

intelligent: smart

land: to strike a blow

lyric: the words of a song

mansion: a very large house

motivation: the will to do something

muscular: made up of large muscles

network: a radio or television company that produces programs for broadcast

nominate: to name someone for an award or a position

offend: to make someone feel hurt or angry

Oscar: an award given to actors, directors, designers, etc.

outspoken: speaking in a bold way

portray: to play the role of; to act as

producer: a person who oversees or pays to create a TV show or film

promote: to tell others about something in order to sell it

recording contract: an agreement to record music for a fee

represent: to show

respect: a feeling of honor or regard

review: a piece of writing or a TV or radio report that gives an opinion about a new book, movie, play, etc.

rhythm: the movement or flow of sounds in a pattern

sequel: the next movie or book in a series

single: a recording having one short tune on each side

supportive: encouraging; helpful

theme song: the main song in a movie, play, or TV show

time slot: the period of time when a TV show is broadcast

translate: to put into words other people can understand

versatile: changing easily

Bibliography

Anderson, Marilyn D. *Will Smith*. People in the News. San Diego: Lucent Books, 2003.

Greene, Meg. *Will Smith*. Galaxy of Superstars. Philadelphia: Chelsea House Publishers, 2002.

Marron, Maggie. *Will Smith: From Rap Star to Mega Star*. New York: Warner Books, 2000.

McCracken, Kristin. *Will Smith*. Celebrity Bios. New York: Children's Press, 2000.

Muldufsky, Peri and Ariel. *Will Smith*. Kansas City, Mo.: Andrews McMeel Publishing, 1998.

Smith, Will. *Just the Two of Us*. New York: Scholastic, 2001.

Solomon, Ed. *Men In Black: The Script and the Story Behind the Film*. Newmarket Pictorial Moviebook. New York: Newmarket Press, 1997.

Useful Addresses

Will Smith
c/o Columbia Records
550 Madison Avenue
New York, NY 10022-3211

Internet Sites

The Biography Channel: Will Smith
http://www.biography.com/search/
article.do?id=9542165

Performing Artists @ My Hero
http://www.myhero.com/myhero/go/directory/
directory.asp?dir=artist

Index

acting, 6–7, 19–20, 22, 25, 26, 28–30, 33–35

Ali, 6, 7, 34–35, 43

Ali, Muhammad, 5, 6, 34–35

Ali, Tatyana, 20

Bad Boys, 26, 42

Big Willie Style, 32, 37, 43

Born to Reign, 38

family, 8–9, 36–37

Fresh Prince, 12, 14, 16, 34

"Gettin' Jiggy Wit It," 32

"Girls Ain't Nuthin' But Trouble," 14, 42

Golden Globe award nomination, 22, 42

Grammy award, 15, 42

grandmother, 40

He's the DJ, I'm the Rapper, 14–15, 42

In This Corner, 18

Independence Day, 28, 42

"Just the Two of Us," 32, 37

Just the Two of Us, 37

Lawrence, Martin, 26

Medina, Benny, 19

Men In Black, 29–30, 32, 33, 38, 42

"Men In Black," 32, 43

Men In Black II, 38

"Miami," 32, 43

Oscar nomination, 35, 43

"Parents Just Don't Understand," 15

Pinkett, Jada, 37, 43

rap, 10–11, 12, 14–15, 18, 32, 40, 42

school, 9

Smith, Jaden, 37

Smith, Trey, 37

Smith, Willow, 37

Spielberg, Steven, 29

Sugar Hill Gang, 10

The Fresh Prince of Bel-Air, 19, 20, 22, 25, 42

Townes, Jeff (DJ Jazzy Jeff), 12, 14, 16, 18, 42

Where the Day Takes You, 25, 42